Tears in His Bottle

Linda Prescott-Precise

WESTBOW
PRESS*
A DIVISION OF THOMAS NELSON
& ZONDERVAN

Scripture quotations marked (NIV) are taken from the Holy Bible, New International Version®, NIV®. Copyright © 1973, 1978, 1984, 2011 by Biblica, Inc.™ Used by permission of Zondervan. All rights reserved worldwide.

Scripture taken from the Holy Bible, NEW INTERNATIONAL READERS VERSION®, NIrV® Copyright © 1973, 1978, 1984, 2011 by Biblica, Inc.® Used by permission. All rights reserved worldwide

Scripture quotes marked (NKJV) are taken from the New King James Version®. Copyright © 1982 by Thomas Nelson. Used by permission. All rights reserved.

Scripture quotations are taken from the Holy Bible, New Living Translation, copyright ©1996, 2004, 2007, 2013, 2015 by Tyndale House Foundation. Used by permission of Tyndale House Publishers, Inc., Carol Stream, Illinois 60188. All rights reserved

WestBow Press books may be ordered through booksellers or by contacting:

WestBow Press
A Division of Thomas Nelson & Zondervan
1663 Liberty Drive
Bloomington, IN 47403
www.westbowpress.com
1 (866) 928-1240

ISBN: 978-1-5127-8570-8 (sc)
ISBN: 978-1-5127-8569-2 (e)

Library of Congress Control Number: 2017906442

Print information available on the last page.

WestBow Press rev. date: 05/04/2017

Preface

You keep track of all my sorrows. You have collected all my tears in your bottle. You have recorded each one in your book. (Psalm 56:8)

These words came alive in my heart when I was a very young girl. They gave me hope during times when I felt abandoned and alone. At times, I would hear and obey God, and He would rescue me. Then there were those other times when I would try to go it alone. It is my hope that my story will encourage you during your trials in life and inspire you to always look for God in all your circumstances and seek His wisdom and direction. His word promises that He does keep track of all our sorrows and He really does have all your tears in His bottle. What an awesome God!

Dedicated to my precious children, Don, Christy, and Paul, and to my dear husband, Joe, who inspired me to tell my story. I love all of you.

Chapter 1

*G*rowing up at my house was simple. "Keep your mouth shut, and don't break the rules as outlined by Mother." Simple rules also included, "Don't sit on your bed after it is made, eat all your food, and never question or complain about anything."

Dad worked hard all day in his dental lab, and Mother helped him. On the weekends, Dad would stay drunk, and Mom would scream, throw fits, and cry. I stayed in my room as a young child and stayed gone as a teenager. I never had friends because I could never bring them home, and I couldn't visit them as I might talk about family matters. Mother and Dad argued about everything. Mother did most of the yelling and screaming, and Dad would just get another drink and ignore her.

Mom didn't live in the real world. She saw herself as a sophisticated lady who liked to wear nice clothes and always had every hair in place with her makeup applied perfectly. She was a pretty woman, and I suspect she was disappointed that she was the wife of a dental technician instead of a dentist or doctor. I was always amused when someone rang our doorbell. She would be fussing and yelling, but when she opened the door, she became another person. She was soft-spoken, with a big smile, and was so gracious—hardly that screaming, hateful woman we saw behind the door. I never figured out if she yelled because he drank or he drank because she yelled. All I knew was that we didn't live like Ozzie and Harriet of TV fame.

I walked alone, five blocks every Sunday morning, to attend Sunday school and church at the Jefferson Avenue Baptist Church. One Sunday morning, I gave my life to Jesus, and I was baptized that same Sunday night. My parents weren't there, as they were having a party at our house and everyone was drinking and playing cards. I don't know if they ever realized I even left the house alone and walked those five blocks to the church on that night. I began to learn then that I had a friend in Jesus. I talked to Him every day about everything.

A few months later, we moved to another state. I was twelve years old. I didn't get to go to church anymore. I began to drift away from my friend Jesus. I was a quiet girl who did not make friends easily.

I was the third child of four. I made good grades and was on the student council and a cheerleader in junior high and high school. My younger sister had epilepsy and had serious seizures every day. I was given the responsibility of looking after her and had to take her with me when I went anywhere. My older brother was charged with looking after me. He often told me that we were not being raised by our parents, but we were just growing up on our own. As I reflect on my growing years, I realize that my brother was right. We were taught to be clean and to be quiet, but no one taught us the real things we needed to know to get through life. My older sister left home at seventeen. She married a soldier and never returned. She was six years older than me. My brother married at twenty-one and moved away also.

I was a dreamer. I daydreamed about being a wife and mother. I would live in a big, beautiful house, and my children would be beautiful and perfect. My husband would be handsome and successful, and we would go to church every Sunday and be respected people.

Chapter 2

When I was fifteen, we were evicted from our home, and all our furniture and even our car was repossessed. We had to move again. We moved back to the city where I was born because my dad's family lived there. They rented a furnished home for us and loaned my dad an old car.

I was so lonely. I had one girl friend I had known as a young girl. I missed my old school, being a cheerleader, and feeling like I was somewhat important. Now I was a nobody. I hated every day of school and never felt that I belonged.

My friend arranged a blind date with a young soldier who was a friend of her boyfriend. I was smitten with him and thought he liked me too. I was a mature young lady, and my body reflected that. I had not dated very much and was still a virgin. I was hungry for attention and affection. We saw each other every day. We met in mid-December. By mid-March, I knew I was pregnant. I did not dare tell my parents. He was four years older, and his parents told him he should marry me. We ran away to Georgia and got married.

I knew I had made a big mistake within the first few days. We went to a hardware store to purchase a lock for the front door of our little cottage. We were wandering through the store, and I stopped to look at towel holder when I saw him slip a lock into his pocket. I was shocked and very upset with him. After we left the store, I confronted him. He became very angry. He slapped me across my face. From that moment on, if I said or did anything he didn't like, he would hit me.

When I was eight months pregnant, I went to my parents and told them he was beating me. My mother looked at me sternly and said, "You burned your butt. Now you sit on the blister!" I knew then that I could never go home or seek help from my parents. I needed to lean on Jesus again.

By the time our baby was born, I had sported several black eyes and a broken nose. He had an affair with a lady in his office, and when I confronted him, he slapped me again and told me to stay out of his business.

I stayed in that marriage for twenty years and had three children. Jesus became my closest friend. We moved nineteen times in twenty years, and there was no time for friends. The beatings were severe at times, and at other times, he would just slap me or knock me down.

I cannot find the words to tell you what those twenty years did to my self-esteem. He was verbally and physically abusive. He once broke a bottle over my head and stomped my legs while wearing his combat boots. I was knocked unconscious, and when I came to my senses, there was a large clot of blood on the floor by my head. I was very afraid and asked him to take me to the hospital, but he refused. There would be too many questions and he might get in trouble, so he put a cold compress on my head and put me to bed. If I received a bad beating, he would not allow me to leave the house till all visible signs were gone. I was never allowed any access to money, except when he would decide he could trust me to go buy groceries or clothing for the kids.

We had three children, and they were now old enough to see and understand how abusive their father could be. He beat them and threatened them. We could never talk to anyone about what went on in our home.

He rose to the rank of major in the army. We always had

a nice home, and I had my beautiful children. He became an alcoholic and more abusive than ever. I had many black eyes, cuts, and bruises. He began to beat me in places where the bruises wouldn't show. Some years were worse than others. I never went more than three months without being beaten. He would always ask me why I made him do that to me. He often said, "Who is going to believe you? You are just another spoiled housewife who wants the army to support you. If they had wanted me to have a wife and kids, they would have issued them to me." He would continually tell me how stupid I was and that he would fix my face so no other man would ever want me.

Just when I would think I could not bear it another minute, he would get orders for Vietnam or Korea and be gone for a year, and we would all get a vacation from him. And then another year would pass.

Chapter 3

*Y*ou must be asking yourself, "Why didn't she leave then?" I can only tell you that when you are beaten and talked down to for so many years, you have no self-esteem and certainly no confidence in your own abilities. How would I support my children? Where could we go to hide from him? He said he would never let me go and would never allow me to have custody of our children. We had been married twenty years when he got orders for Korea. My older two children had left home. My oldest son went into the army, and my daughter married. My youngest son was ten years old. My father had passed away, and I had gone to work to help pay my mother's bills.During this time, I came to the realization that the only way my life would ever change was to let him know that I would not allow him to abuse me anymore. I wrote him a letter and told him that if he ever hit me again, I would divorce him. He did not respond to my letter. He had been home eight days when the beating happened. It was severe, blackening both of my eyes, breaking my nose, and cracking my jawbone. He didn't object to going to a lawyer. I thought that was strange, but I was so thankful to see the end of this marriage that I didn't hesitate to call the lawyer. The nightmare would be over.

He did not contest the conditions of the divorce. His only desire was to keep our home. We owned another home that my mom lived in, and I didn't want to move her. I had never had a happy day in our home anyway. I wanted my car, $10,000 cash, and some of the furniture and things that I would need in my new home.

My face was such a battered mess as we sat before the lawyer that he had no choice but to comply with all my requests. I learned a few weeks later that he had brought a Korean woman to the States, and he married her as soon as the divorce was final. Now I understood why he did not object to the divorce and why he wanted the house. My nightmare was finally over, and the Korean lady could have him with my blessing.

Chapter 4

*N*ow I had new challenges: How would I support my young son and take care of my mom? The $750 a month in child support seemed like a lot. But I also had my widowed mother to care for. My mom and my dad had both accepted Jesus in their sixties, and I was thrilled when that happened. I knew I would have to make enough money to help take care of my mom and my young son. I spent most of that first night crying and praying. I was working now, but with two black eyes and so many bruises, I was too ashamed to go back to work yet. My boss was a kind lady, and when I told her what I was enduring, she gave me the time off I needed to heal and get myself together.

I felt so sad. I had dreamed of being free for so long, yet this new freedom scared me. Could I survive on my own? Would there be enough money to care for my mom and my son? The furniture store where I was working was going out of business in thirty days. What would I do then? Could I get another job? I had so many questions and fears.

Although I had given my heart to Jesus and was saved, I had not been discipled. I had not read or practiced enough of God's word to know what being a Christian meant. I had not read all His promises. I did not understand what it meant to surrender everything to Him. I only knew that He was my friend and I could call out to Him and He would help me as He had done so many times over the past twenty-five years of my life. How wonderful it would have been if I could have recalled even a few of His promises, like Isaiah 41:10: "Don't be afraid, for I am with you. Don't be discouraged, for I am your God. I will strengthen you and help you. I will hold you up with My victorious right hand" (NLT). Wow! What a difference that word from my Jesus would have made in my level of fear and confusion at that moment in my life.

But even in my ignorance, God was faithful and recognized the sincere humility of my heart and heard my prayers. I told God I would work hard and that I wasn't looking for a handout. I just asked for a chance at a decent job that would pay enough to take care of my family.

At last, I was healed enough to go back to work. Being busy and being with people encouraged me. The following day, a gentleman came into the store. I knew this man, as he came by regularly to pick up copy for the store's TV commercials. That day, he picked up his copy points and then came over to talk with me. My boss had told him about my divorce and how I had been beaten. He was a kind and godly man, and he asked me if I had a job when the store closed. I told him that I did not. He told me he knew my situation and wanted to help me. He asked me if I would like to work in television. Television? Sounded interesting! I asked what I would be doing, and he said I would be selling commercials instead of furniture. I was very excited, even though I did not understand just what I might be doing. I asked him how much it paid, and he smiled and said, "Much more than you are making now." He told me to be at the station the next morning as he had told them about me and they would be expecting me.

Well, friends, I can tell you honestly that the only thing I knew about TV was how to turn on one. I was scared and excited. Boy, did God and I ever talk that night! I told God I would work hard, and if He would go before me and give me wisdom, I would be faithful to give Him all the glory for any success I might have. I knew God heard my prayers. God answered my prayers! I went through that interview with confidence and grace. My God was with me. I got the job.

My office was forty-four miles from my home. Each morning, I would talk to God all the way to the office. I spent the first two weeks learning all I would need to know to make calls on clients. The sales manager said I needed to make a minimum of ten calls a day if I wanted to succeed. I did just that. I would never go back to the office until I had seen at least ten clients. I was an overnight success. In ninety days, I was their top sales person and received a $1,500 bonus. I was on cloud nine. It was December, and I stopped on my way home and bought the biggest Christmas tree that they could tie to my car! I told my young son to make his Christmas list. He was happy and excited too. He didn't see his father anymore. He took his new wife and moved to Korea, and none of us ever saw or heard from him again.

I had been on my job about six months when the manager approached me about doing a daily talk show in addition to my sales job. Why not? Everything I touched was turning to success and money. The show led to appearances in commercials and more benefits. People knew and recognized me wherever I went, and soon I was promoted to sales manager. I realized that when God is leading and directing your life, anything can happen. I was not that beaten-down and frightened woman any longer.

Chapter 5

Two years later, I met and married a sweet and very handsome man who loved me, and life was good. He had a young son, and he came to live with us. We raised our young sons together. God had taken a little "nobody" girl who had no special skills or talent and certainly no self-confidence and given her a life she had only dreamed about. God was opening doors to a life I had never thought possible. I was very happy. I was treated with dignity and respect wherever I went. Clients were kind and acted as if I was someone important. To make my life complete, we went to church as a family.

But this was only the beginning. After eight years with that company, the sales manager job led to a bigger job offer. A very rich businessman who owned a chain of radio and TV stations called and wanted to talk with me. I had never met this man, but I had certainly heard about him. My husband and I talked about it, and he encouraged me to talk with the man, even though he did have quite a reputation as being hard and demanding.

The morning of the interview, I woke up very early and got on my knees. I sure wouldn't take a chance on any kind of job unless I felt God was in it and was moving me in that direction. I asked God to lead me through the interview and give me the words I needed to speak. I also asked Him to give me a red flag if I should decline the position. I asked Him to let everything flow smoothly if this was a place He wanted me to work. I did not want to be out of His will.

I had no idea what the job was or how much it paid. I had heard he was looking for a sales manager for his big country station. I was very uneasy about working for him. What if I gave up the good job I had and it didn't work out? I was uneasy in my spirit. As soon as I entered his office, I could feel the pains of fear in my stomach. Was God showing me His will? I was ready to run! He was sitting behind a grand desk in a luxurious leather chair. He had been badly burned in an airplane crash in the war, and much of his face was disfigured. I was afraid to look at him. But when he spoke to me, God took over. The interview could not have gone better. He voice was kind and soft. He told me he had heard about me from my peers, and I was just the kind of person he liked to employ. Then he asked me how much money it would take for me to come to work for him. I had not even thought about being asked this question. I gulped and blurted out an amount that was $8,000 per year more than I was making on my present job. I never dreamed he would oblige me. As it turned out, I would be making about $60,000 to start and eventually even more than that. The job was the position of sales manager of his big country station.

After talking with him, my uneasiness and fear of him began to subside. In addition to the pay raise, he also bought me a Lincoln Town Car and paid for all my gas and dry cleaning and to have my hair done each week. Not bad for this young woman who had spent the first twenty years of her adult life hiding in the house crying, with black eyes and a bruised body and too ashamed to tell anyone.

During these years, I got serious about my relationship with God. I attended church regularly and had daily devotional time with God. I talked to Him every day and sometimes, all day long. I now had much of His word buried in my heart and could call it up when I needed reassurance in any area of my life. I prayed daily for God's wisdom as I realized that God put me in the job and God would direct me. I knew I could not have accomplished any of this without divine intervention.

The radio station grew into a multimillion-dollar operation. I was respected in our community and given many accolades. I stayed in that job for eight years and became vice president of his communications company and general manager of his very large country station. It was a very demanding job, and he would call at midnight or 4:00 a.m. to ask me to do something for him or write a check to settle a lawsuit. He was quite a character, but he was always respectful to me. He spent money as if it grew on trees and eventually lost his radio and TV stations except for the big country station I was managing. He gave me a contract and guaranteed my employment and benefits when I was ready to retire. Of course, contracts meant nothing to him as he was experienced at breaking contracts and getting folks to settle out of court. I should have known I would be no exception. I had done and was doing a good job for him. The station was consistently number one in the ratings, and the revenue had more than doubled under my leadership. I was financially set for life.

Chapter 6

I continued to grow in my relationship with the Lord and went to church and to retreats and conferences whenever possible. I had become very active in my own church and in the women's ministries. In late January of 1997, I attended a weekend retreat. As a ministry team leader, I was there to counsel women who would be experiencing God for the first time or feeling that God was speaking to them in some special way. God met me there. I was overwhelmed with the sense of His presence. I didn't understand what God was calling me to do, but I knew He was calling me to serve Him in a new way. I knew, too, that managing a country radio station was no longer in His plan. I remember telling Him that I would do whatever He called me to do. In the months to come, everything in my life began to change. We sold our big house in the country and moved into town.

My boss began to treat me differently. He questioned all my decisions and wanted daily reports of everything we were selling and to know of any personnel problems or changes. This would have been reasonable if he had always done this, but prior to this, he never wanted to know about anything except how much money was in the bank and how much he could spend. I talked with God several times a day. The experience with God at the retreat would not leave my mind.

I felt God wanted me to leave my job. The stress from the

continual pressures my boss placed on me were getting very intense. I tried to talk to my husband about it, and he asked me if I was crazy. Why would I want to quit such a lucrative job? He did not believe God would lead me to do that. One Wednesday morning, I said, "God, surely You don't expect me to quit my job?" But in my heart, I knew He wanted me to do exactly that! I was not at the point where I would be obedient. I am ashamed to tell you that I didn't trust God to take care of me and my family. I was making more money than most men I knew. We were enjoying the good life that money can buy. What was God thinking? Ever been there?

I wanted to tell God to come up with another plan, because this one was just not acceptable. I argued with God until it was time to go to work. When I got to work, I was very uneasy in my spirit. The day drug on, and everything seemed to be normal, so I thought I must be overreacting.

Around three that afternoon, my secretary buzzed me and said our company lawyer was there to see me. He was also a friend, so I wasn't alarmed that he had stopped in to visit. His office was just across the street. He might have wanted free tickets to a concert we were hosting the next week. He came in, and after exchanging greetings, He told me my boss had called him and I needed to get my purse and call someone to pick me up as I was fired. I asked why, and he said he did not need a reason, that he had just decided to make some changes. I could see the pain in his eyes. He did not want to deliver this news. My boss was a coward and could not fire folks. He always had me or our attorney do that for him. I was not to remove any papers or anything from my office. He escorted me out of the office, and another employee took me home. I remember that I kept saying, "Please don't let me hurt my witness for You, Lord." I said this many times over the next few days. I did not want to say ugly words about my boss or the company I had loved so much over the past eight years. I left with my dignity intact—no tears, no good-byes.

When I got to church the following Sunday, the preacher and some folks who worked with me had told everyone that I was fired because I was a Christian and always stood for Christian principles. Well, that sounded good to me and made the pain more bearable. God was still taking care of me, because by then, I was feeling pretty angry and could have said a lot of ugly things about my former boss. But God, in His mercy, struck me with the worst case of laryngitis I have ever had. I could not utter a word! God honored my prayer about honoring my witness for Him. I still don't know the reason I was fired. A man who was a friend to my boss took over my job. I think that may have been the reason. When you are not obedient to what God is telling you to do, God will still accomplish His will. My friend Jesus was teaching me another lesson. If I had been obedient I could have saved myself the humiliation of being fired. But I was more interested in hanging on to my new life with all the money and prestige. I did not realize that God had graciously provided me those years in broadcasting to prepare me to serve Him in ministry and not to make me rich.

Chapter 7

There was a group of Christian businessmen in town who had wanted to start a contemporary Christian radio station. They wanted it to be a non-profit and to be a real ministry to our area. They had contacted me several times after my retreat and wanted to hire me, but soon learned they could not afford me (my words). As I reflect on this time in my life, I can clearly see that God was trying to move me into this radio ministry. My greed and rebellion would not let me see this. Satan was having his way with my life.

They had started the station, but it was failing miserably. They had been on the air about sixty days and could not get people who had experience to work for them as they had little money to pay them. My firing was great news to them! They called and offered me $24,000 to start—a far cry from what I had been earning. But it was more than the unemployment check I was getting. After more praying and more tears, I took the job. By this time, I knew, as that group of men knew, that God was directing my steps and theirs.

When I tell you that this was the hardest job I ever had, I would not be exaggerating at all. I found a retired disc jockey who agreed to work for a small salary as he already had a retirement income. We began the process of trying to build a radio station that would be a ministry to our community. We had no on-air personnel and no salespeople or fundraisers.

He and I became the station. We did the morning show, and I would go out and try to sell our programming. We had a part-time lady in the office to answer the phones and do all the paperwork. I also had to do all the documentation to send to the government to get our nonprofit status.

I became very close to the Lord. He was my lifeline! We prayed every day and some days we prayed continually! The board of directors agreed to put money in if we got in a real bind but made it clear that they expected the station to pay for itself. I prayed in the money for the payroll, the electric bill, the telephone bill, and all the other mountains of bills that come with a radio station that wants to succeed. I would bring the bills home and lay hands on them and pray. I never asked for more than we needed. The next day, the mail would contain enough checks or someone would walk in off the street and give us a check to cover the bills.

At first, it was just enough to cover the expense, and then we would thank God, and soon He began to send more than just what our daily need was.

Every day became a lesson in learning to listen for, and listen to, what God was saying to me.

One morning I was on my way to work, and I was whining to the Lord. I was telling Him how hard this job was and how much I hated it and that there was never enough money. Some weeks I couldn't even pay myself. Whine, whine, whine—I had gotten good at it! There was a song playing on the radio (my station) about a little baby talking to his mother from heaven and telling her how he still loved her even though she had aborted him. I began to cry, and God began to speak to my heart.

God told me that I didn't begin to know what He was doing through that little Christian radio station. He was changing lives and healing hearts of people I would never meet. He had big plans for that little station.

When I got to work, a young woman called me and told

me she had been on her way to the abortion clinic when she heard that song on the radio. She changed her mind and was going to have that baby. I connected her to a local organization that believed in the sanctity of human life to help her. I was beginning to see and understand why God had led me into the world of broadcasting.

My new vocation became a way of life that I was very proud of and opened the doors of speaking and teaching to many people. God was using me for His glory and not my own.

The next five years were filled with new experiences and opportunities to minister to many people. The station grew in listeners and in revenue, and a big broadcasting company bought the station. I stayed on for several more years, but my husband's health began to fail and we wanted more time together, so I retired.

Chapter 8

A few months after I retired, God presented me with the challenge of my life.

My daughter called me and said she thought she had a bad case of the flu. She had been to the emergency room twice but they had not done much for her. She sounded very weak. I went over and checked on her and could see that she was very ill. I brought her home with me so I could take care of her. She was married, but her husband worked full time and did not seem interested in caring for her. She had already been sick for several weeks. I tried the usual chicken soup mixed with Mom's tender loving care, but two days later she continued to get worse. I loaded her up, took her to another hospital, and announced to them that I would not be leaving until she was diagnosed and treated. They admitted her and began running tests.

She was very ill. A few days later, the doctors met with me and told me she had a very serious infection. They were giving her mega doses of antibiotics. Her body was not responding to all the medicine as quickly as they had hoped. They placed her in a long-term care area of the hospital. Her husband came to see her once a week for about an hour. I was there every day. She seemed to be getting better, and after five weeks, the doctor said she could go home. My husband and I went to the hospital to bring her home.

When we walked in her room, I was shocked to see her condition. She was very lethargic and appeared to be very drowsy. The doctor came in and said he had decided she was not ready to go home as all her blood work indicated she was relapsing. He left the room, and she asked me to help her to the restroom. When we got in the restroom, she began to fall. I caught her and screamed for help. The nurses got her to the bed and began calling for help. They took my husband and I to a small office down the hall but I could hear them calling for "code blue" for her room number.

I was terrified. It seemed like forever before the doctor finally came in to talk to us. I think it was about an hour later. He said she had coded twice and was now on life support in the critical care unit. He was a Christian doctor and recognized me from the Christian radio station. He prayed with us. He said we could see her in a little while when they got her cleaned up.

Sometime after midnight, we finally got to go in for a few minutes to see her. It is difficult for me to convey to you all the things I was thinking and feeling during that long evening. To the doctors and nurses, she was a young woman. (She was in her forties.) But to me, this was my baby girl. My only daughter! Surely God would not allow her to die! She looked so helpless and lifeless laying there. I sobbed uncontrollably. My husband tried to comfort me, but my heart was so filled with fear that I could not think clearly. Finally, Satan had me in a position where I was so frozen with fear that I *could not* call for my friend Jesus.

The days passed, and each day I sat in the waiting room till I could go in to see her. There was no improvement. She was not getting better. She was totally unresponsive.

One evening, the doctor came to me and told me they needed to do open-heart surgery on her right away as the infection had severely damaged the main aorta valve in her heart. He asked my permission to proceed. I asked him when he planned to operate, and he said right now! He disappeared behind the big ICU doors, and a little while later, they wheeled her into surgery. The waiting was agonizing.

The surgery took four or five hours. Many friends from our church were there with us and praying for her recovery. I could not pray. I could only cry and call out the name of Jesus. In the wee hours of the morning, the doctor came to tell us that the heart valve replacement was a success.

I was so happy and relieved. We thought she would get off life support. He said no. She was still in critical condition. The days seemed to pass so slowly.

A few weeks later, I arrived at the hospital, and she was off the machine and talking. I was shocked and so happy! This nightmare was over!

Her only son was seventeen years old, and he was there to tell her he was going to the prom. She was happy and excited and made him promise to come to the hospital with his date before the prom so she could see them in their prom clothes. That evening he kept his word and showed off for his mother. She was proud and happy, even though she was still very sick.

I went home that night with a great sense of relief and feeling like the end was in sight.

But God had other plans.

When I arrived at the hospital the next morning, she had been put back on life support. She had coded again during the night. Would this ever end? The days wore on.One afternoon, her heart doctor came to talk with us. "We need to think of turning off her machine,as she can have no quality of life. We don't know what else we could do to treat her." I could not consider such a thought. The tears would not stop. My heart was breaking. I could not bury my only daughter! God could not possibly expect such a sacrifice from me. I had been living a Christian life. I was teaching Sunday school and speaking to women everywhere about God's saving grace and mercy. Dear God, where was my mercy? I could not give up my daughter.

My only daughter! I thought I could earn God's mercy. The Lord still had so much to teach me!

I tried to sleep that night, but I wrestled with God all night. He reminded me of His sacrifice of His Son, Jesus. He allowed Him to die a horrible death on the cross so I and people like me could have the opportunity to receive the gift of eternal life. Now I was feeling ashamed of myself. How could I dare to think that I deserved to keep my daughter when He had sacrificed His Son? My daughter was a Christian and would go to heaven when she died. Maybe He wanted to use her death to save her husband and her children or her brothers. I could not possibly know or understand God's plan or negotiate or earn His favor.

One thing I knew for certain was that God was walking with me through this crisis. Jeremiah 29:11 says, "'For I know the plans I have for you' says the Lord. 'They are plans for good and not for disaster, to give you a future and a hope'" (NLT).

God's promises and the many scriptures He had hidden in my heart came alive in me. My God had not forsaken me. He was still right there with me. He was teaching and leading me for His purpose and not my own.

When morning came, my husband and I knelt in our living room, and we told God that if He wanted our daughter, it was okay. I told him that I loved her and did not want to give her up, but if this was in His plan that I trusted His wisdom and asked Him to please give me the strength to deal with it.

I felt a sense of peace in my heart. A burden had been lifted.

Before I went to the hospital that morning, I decided to send an e-mail to the church and update our situation. We were flooded with e-mails every day from folks who were praying for her. I opened an e-mail from a sweet friend I did not see often, but I knew she was a prayer warrior. All the e-mail said was, "Read James 5:13–15 (NIV)."

I opened my bible to James 5:13–15 and read these words:

> Is anyone among you in trouble? Let them pray.
> Is anyone happy? Let them sing songs of praise.
> Is anyone among you sick? Let them call for the
> elders of the church to pray over him and anoint
> him with oil in the name of the Lord. And the
> prayer offered in faith will make the sick person
> well; the Lord will raise him up. If they have
> sinned, they will be forgiven.

I read it again and again. I took my Bible to the hospital and sat there in the waiting room and read it over and over. The words became alive in my heart. I did not recall ever reading these scriptures before. Now they were in my heart! God was talking to me. He was telling me exactly what to do.

But I am a slow learner.

One of our associate pastors showed up in the waiting room to sit with me and pray with me. I asked him to read James 5:13-15. He did. I asked, "Do you think this is true? Does God really heal people?" He asked me, "What do you believe? Do you believe it is true?" I told him "If God said it then I believe it!"

He gave me his cell phone and said, "Call the church, and let's get some folks here to lay hands on her and ask for her healing."

That evening, several deacons and men from our church and a senior pastor came to the hospital, and my husband and I took them to her room. With the anointing oil, the senior pastor made the sign of the cross on her forehead. Each man laid hands on her and prayed prayers of healing over her. I wept. It was a tender and beautiful moment.

I knew in my heart that I had heard from God and that I was following in obedience.

She did not wake up or show any indication that anything

different was happening. What was God doing? I went home that night, and even though I could see no visible change in the situation, I felt a peace in my heart. She was in God's care now, and it was not up to me to second-guess the great Physician. I slept peacefully that night.

Chapter 9

The next day was Friday. I arrived at the hospital around 9:00 a.m. as I usually did. There were no signs of change. I was sitting in the waiting room, and around noon, her doctor came to me and said, "I don't know why, but there are some big improvements in Christy's numbers, and a few minutes ago, her kidneys began to function on their own and shut down the dialysis machine. If she keeps improving like this, she could be off life support and in a room in a few days!"

I knew what had happened! I told her doctor, and he rejoiced with me and reminded me that sometimes doctors don't have all the answers. He reminded me that God is still the great Healer.

Well, that was Friday, and Tuesday she came off that machine, and on Friday she was moved to a private room. It was her birthday! Our God is an awesome God! He had walked with me through all those terrifying days and nights, and even when I could not pray, He loved me and took care of me and my daughter. He had given me a modern-day miracle, and I knew He wanted me to tell others that He was still on His throne and He hears and answers our prayers.

Today she is happy, working as an accounting clerk, and serving God with a smile that would melt your heart and a witness for the love and mercy of God to everyone she encounters.

Psalm 56:8 says that God has all my tears in a bottle. I believe that. Furthermore, I believe God saves those tears and at the appropriate time, He pours those tears out on me as blessings. Think about what He tells us in Romans 8:28: "And we know that God causes everything to work together for the good of those who love God and are called, according to His purpose for them" (NLT).

As I look back over my life, I realize that God has always been there, and He knows all my sorrows and truly kept all my tears in His bottle. I don't deserve such mercy, nor have I done anything in my life to earn such grace, but because God loves me and I am His daughter, He chooses to lavish such mercy and love on me.

Friends, my God knows my name, and He knows your name. Isaiah 49:16 says, "See, I have written your name on the palms of My hands" (NLT).

Chapter 10

We settled into our retirement years and enjoyed traveling and having fun with our friends from church.

My husband's heart problems continued to worsen. He always called me "Shug," and many folks at church thought that was my name. He truly loved life and loved his family. He loved me, and even though he was not a romantic man or prone to show much affection, I knew he loved me and that I could depend on him. He knew he could always count on me to be there for him.

He had a heart attack in the early years of our marriage that did a good bit of damage to his heart. He was hospitalized once or twice every year following his open-heart surgery. He had twelve stints in his heart. That did not dampen his spirit or ever cause him to indulge in self-pity. He would tell you quick that he was fine and there were many people much worse off than him. His heart problems were quite serious, and both of us were always on guard if he had any unusual symptoms or pain he had not previously known.

We had been married about thirty years when new symptoms began to show up. He complained about his stomach hurting. I finally convinced him to go to the doctor. They ran some tests and told us he had colon cancer. We were shocked.

We had always felt his heart would be the cause of his death. We had never even considered any other possibility.

We agreed on a surgeon, and he had the cancerous tumor removed. They said he wouldn't need any radiation or chemo as they had gotten all the cancer. We returned home and began the process of healing.

We were very happy. He had slipped past death once again. Over the years, he had faced near death many times. But God would always spare him, and he would go back to serving in the church and bringing joy and smiles to everyone he encountered.

He wasn't as strong as he had been before the cancer. It took more effort for him to get to church and put on his big smile. We made several trips back to the surgeon, and he would do CAT scans and PET scans and tell us there were some spots on his liver and lungs, but they did not feel they were anything to be concerned about. He had his surgery in March, and the following August, he had another heart attack.

During his stay in the hospital, a doctor came in and asked me who was treating my husband's cancer. I told him that he did not have cancer. He did not argue with me but asked if we would allow an oncologist to look at him. We agreed. The oncologist ordered a liver biopsy and PET scan. Several days later, we went to his office. We knew he probably had cancer. Maybe it would not be advanced. After all, the surgeon had told us they had removed all the cancer. The doctor was very kind. We asked him to tell us how bad it was and what his treatment plan would be and what the prognosis was. My husband had already told me he would not take chemo as he had seen how it wrecked people physically and he wanted no part of it. The doctor laid it all out for us.

He had stage four cancer in his liver, his spleen, and his lungs. With chemo, he might have six to nine months, and without it, maybe three months. I was stunned. I think he was also. How could we tell his children and mine? They loved him, and he was their hero. My heart was broken, and the tears flowed uncontrollably again.

He was stronger. He reassured me that we could get through this and that only God could decide when he would die. The doctor was a Christian and agreed with him. He was to start chemo the next week. I knew he was desperate to be cured since he readily agreed to the chemo treatments. The weeks that followed led us down a short but painful journey. He did well during his first chemo treatment. The treatments were very strong and were scheduled three weeks apart. During his second treatment, he began to have heart problems. They had to stop the treatment. We went to the hospital. He was very sick and very weak. We were in the hospital about five days. All the doctors and hospital staff were so kind and caring. Several doctors came in one morning and told us they had done all they knew to do. He would not live much longer. They sent us home with hospice care. It was mid-September.

Thanksgiving and Christmas were always very special at our house. We always had his three children and their children and my three children and their children, and the house was always full of love and laughter. We loved those holidays. He asked me to put the Christmas tree up before Thanksgiving as he did not feel he could make it till Christmas. With a breaking heart, I did as he asked. Thanksgiving was wonderful even though he could not enjoy much of the food. The kids were in denial about his looming death. I cried and begged God to spare his life, but I knew God had another plan.

About two weeks before he died, I was awakened in the night to the sound of his sobbing. I sat up and asked him what was wrong.He said, "I don't want to die." I asked him if he had talked to God about it, and he told me that God had spared him many times and "You can't make deals with God."

We sat up the rest of the night, talking about our years together, our relationship with God, and our children. I will never forget that night. He told me that I had been the best wife a man could ever hope for and he wanted me to be happy and stay close to God. He told me he was proud of me.

A few weeks later, on December 14, he entered heaven, leaving behind a broken-hearted family. We somehow muddled through the Christmas holidays and prayed for happier days to come in the New Year.

Chapter 11

The days and months following his death just seemed to drag by slowly. I taught Bible studies and Sunday school and did some public speaking. I was so lonely. The days and the nights all seemed the same. The kids were as attentive to me as time permitted. But they all worked and had busy lives.

A sweet couple from my church took me to dinner one evening, and he told me about a part-time job as a test administrator that was available. I applied and was hired. It was the perfect job for me. It would be two or three days a week and have better than average pay. I was still lonely and grieving.

I learned many things as I walked through my daughter's illness and near death and then my husband's cancer and his death. There were so many times I felt the presence and closeness of God. I could literally sense His presence in my spirit. I would go to a private place (usually my closet) and cry out to Him. I would be so afraid of the future and what each day might present.

Dear friends, I need to tell you that when God is all you have, God is truly all you need. His word became so alive in my heart. It was as if He was personally walking with me and talking to my heart continually. He would whisper to me from His word, "Don't be afraid. I am here with you. I know the plans I have for you. I plan to give you hope and a future and when you call out to Me, I will hear your prayers, and I will answer your prayers." Jeremiah 29:11–13 is forever engraved on my heart.

My husband is healed now. He is happy and has no more pain. I am not telling you that I heard God speak these words to me in the physical sense, but I heard Him in my spirit. Those scriptures I had memorized and hidden in my heart came rushing back to me. I would talk to God all day—not out loud, but in my spirit. I learned to go to God with every detail of my life. If it was important to me, it was important to God. I have had some people tell me that we shouldn't bother God with little problems or details of our lives. I would say to them and to you that my God cares about every area of my life, and He knows how quickly and easily Satan can deceive us. I had constant reassurance that God was with me and He was looking after me. He had a plan for my life, and it would be for my good and His glory.

I found myself in God's waiting room again.

I had been very active in our church as a teacher and speaker. I was getting speaking invitations on a regular basis. I loved teaching and speaking to women. The invitations to speak began to dry up. I spoke three or four more times and continued to teach for a few months. I can't explain what was going on in my heart. I didn't want to study or teach. I still loved going to church because that is where all my friends were. I felt safe and loved there. But I just didn't feel that I belonged anywhere. I stepped down as a teacher.

I tried to fill my life with my job. The job was another answer to prayer as I honestly needed the money. My husband had no life insurance and no retirement pension of any kind, so the little money I had in our savings account was all I had to fall back on.

My oldest son came to live with me several months later. I must admit that I had struggled with the decision to let him live with me. He had been seriously addicted to drugs and had been in and out of jail many times. I decided that I needed to talk with my friend Jesus about my decision. As I began to pray, God immediately began to bring back the story of the prodigal son. I thought about that all day and night. I knew what God wanted me to do. He wanted me to show the same unconditional love to my son that He had shown to me.

My son was being released from prison. He had no clothes, no money, and no place to live. I went to pick him up and took him shopping for clothes. Then I treated him to a steak dinner at a fine restaurant. I told him that I loved him and my only rule was that he would attend church with me every Sunday. He agreed. He had always loved music, so I bought him a guitar. His health was gone after being disabled in the military and years of drug abuse. He began to open up to me, and we talked a lot. He helped me with all the yard work and lots of other household duties. He was faithful to attend church.

One day we were talking. He told me that he wanted what I had. I did not know what he was talking about. I asked him what he meant by that. He said, "I want to know God like you do." My heart rejoiced. I had spent twenty years on my knees, praying for him and for this very day! I knew then that God was at work in his heart.

A few weeks later, he renewed his commitment to follow Christ and joined our church. I had told him that God would restore the years that the locusts had eaten. God has done that. He is happily married today, and although he continually battles some serious health issues, he has remained steadfast in his faith. He was more severely abused by his father than my other children. Many of my beatings were in retaliation for trying to protect him from his father.

My youngest son has fought his personal battles too. A family cannot live through a lifetime of abuse and not escape the scars. Not only did I suffer, but each one of my children suffered. They were beaten and abused too. They had also kept their secret all these years because of fear and shame. The older two acted out their pain and frustrations through drugs and alcohol, while my youngest son became the family joker. He was always trying to make other people laugh, while he was crying inside. He didn't show any outward signs of the abuse he endured until he was in his forties. He is still working through the pain of his youth. I know God will carry him through his pain, just as He has carried his brother and sister. God will restore all the locusts have eaten in his life too.

Chapter 12

I know God has more than one bottle full of my tears. I cried myself to sleep many nights. When I was younger, I cried because of the pain I was living through. Then as I began to realize what I had done to my children by remaining with a man who had been so abusive to all of us, I wept enough to fill many bottles with tears.

When I was finally free of the man who had abused us, I tried to bury it all so deep in my heart that I became afraid to let anyone know where I had come from and what I had lived through. He died in Korea a few years after he moved there. I did not have to fear him any longer, and it was just easier to be this new lady executive who was married to a wonderful, handsome man who lived in a nice house in a nice neighborhood. I never talked much about my kids, and I sure never talked about my past. The shame was overwhelming. I was afraid if people knew my past, they would question my sanity and my character. After all, what kind of woman would allow a man to treat her and her children in such a terrible way? My friends were respectable Christian people who came from respected families. They had only read stories or seen TV dramas about women like me. How could I explain the fear and the low self-esteem I had felt?

I did go to the police one time and was told that they did not get involved in domestic disputes. Another time, I went to his commanding officer and was assured that some action would be taken, and he then told my husband that he needed to get me under control before I caused a real problem. That just brought on another beating worse than any I had endured.

You learn to keep quiet and not rock the boat. The guilt and shame continued to grow, and I buried my past even deeper in my heart.

I am not sure when the breakthrough came. The stronger my faith in God became, the more I realized that God had allowed me to experience all these things so I could share my story to help other women and give them hope. I want women to know that God can help them, and today, there are other resources for them. The police will come to your aid, and if you are being physically abused, you should notify them. There are shelters in most cities now if you need a place to hide with your children. Just get out! These men are mentally unhinged, and they aren't going to change. Your children cannot help themselves, and they are dependent on you to free them of the horror of seeing their mother beaten and abused as well as the fear of what will happen to them if they try to help you. I still wake up screaming some nights when the nightmares come and I am living through it all again.

My husband had been dead just over two years when I met and later married a sweet and godly man. We are newlyweds. He was a gift from God. He was a widower who had lost his wife to cancer. We became great friends and soon realized how much we had in common. We shared stories about our mates and their battles with cancer. We both loved the Lord, and we were both very lonely. We would talk for hours about our lives and all God had brought us through. Our children seemed genuinely happy for us. I told him every sordid detail of my life. He loved me despite my past. He convinced me to share my story with the world.

Most of my friends have no idea of the journey I have traveled. I am no longer afraid of being judged by them. I realize that God's judgment is all I should be concerned about. I am older now, and I still bear the scars even though it has been thirty-seven years since God set me free. Did I once love my former husband? I surely did. Did I believe he could and would change and become my prince charming? I did, for a very long time. But that was the daydreamer inside of me. There does come a time when all of us must come face to face with reality and let go of our fairy tale dreams. What my heart wanted and craved and what life had dealt me were far from the fairy tales I wanted to believe in. I don't mean to imply that I have lost faith in impossible dreams. Far from it. My God is a miracle-working God! He performed miracles two thousand years ago, and He is still performing miracles today. The very fact that I am still here and that my children are alive and healthy and happy is a miracle.

My husband is a gentle and loving man who has placed me on a pedestal. Ephesians 5:33 says, "Nevertheless let each one of you in particular so love his own wife as himself and let the wife see that she respects her husband" (NKJV). He lives out the scriptures every day. I have never known such unconditional love. Those tears have become blessings being poured out in my life.

Even today with all the help available, many are still living in fear and intimidation. God did not intend for you to be beaten and abused. Read those scriptures, and memorize God's promises. Remember that we receive supernatural physical energy and strength when we claim God's promise in Isaiah 40:29-31:

He gives power to the weak,strength to the powerless.

> Even youths will become weak and tired, and young men will fall to exhaustion. But those who trust in the Lord will find new strength. They will soar high on wings like eagles. They will run and not grow weary. They will walk and not faint. (NLT)

I know where my help comes from. You will find our Lord is faithful and His words are true and trustworthy. "You keep track of all my sorrows. You have all my tears in your bottle. You have recorded each one in your book"(Psalm 56:8 NLT). God's word is alive and brings new life to each of us. I once thought I had to solve all my problems. I have learned that I have a friend in Jesus, and He is always watching and listening.

Chapter 13

I am in the last semester in my life now. I want it to be the best ever. I can never repay God for all He has done for me, but I can share my story with others, in hopes that they will turn to Him and let Him guide their lives. All He has asked of me is to tell my story to help others. That is what He wants from you as well. We all have a story. Share your story. Pray about who to share it with and when. God will do the rest. You don't have to be a gifted speaker. God will give you the words.

Don't concern yourself with what others will think or say about you. Only God's opinion matters. Don't allow guilt and shame to imprison you. If you are being abused, pray first and then tell someone. Don't just tell a girlfriend; tell someone who can help you or get you the help you need. Don't stay in an abusive marriage for the sake of your children. You are not helping them. The emotional scars they will carry will be far worse than the pain of a divorce.I am not endorsing divorce. But God has shown me that there are times when it is biblically justified.God's word will guide you. One of my favorite Bible passages is in Ephesians 6:11-18:

> Put on the full armor of God so that you can
> take your stand against the devil's schemes. ...
> Stand firm then, with the belt of truth buckled

around your waist, with the breastplate of righteousness in place, and with your feet fitted with the readiness that comes from the gospel of peace. In addition to all this, take up the shield of faith, with which you can extinguish all the flaming arrows of the evil one. Take the helmet of salvation and the sword of the spirit, which is the word of God. And pray in the spirit on all occasions with all kinds of prayers and requests.

Notice that God does not give us armor for our backs! That is because He always has our backs!

We are to continue to move forward, without looking back or concerning ourselves with the past or what is behind us. God has all of that covered. Tell your story, my friend. Let God decide how and when He will use it. He does not allow us to endure pain and suffering without purpose. He has a plan and a purpose for all our life experiences. God is a loving and forgiving God. He truly has all our tears in His bottle. We can know no greater love! Turn to Him now and ask for His forgiveness and direction. He is there for you, and He will not fail you.

The End

Printed in the United States
By Bookmasters